THE SUCC___ __

BY RAYMOND VAUGHN

The greatest achievement a person can obtain is to reach their full potential and become the person they are capable of becoming!

Special thanks to Darian Holt for challenging me to do something great with my life. He could see the potential for my life that was being restrained and prevented from developing naturally. May this bring about a change in my life that makes him feel that I achieved that goal. It has been a remarkable experience working on this book.

Special thanks to Lisa Gerage Kistler for believing encouraging me to become more than what I was currently being by believing in my potential. She

persuaded me to do more and be more. When I felt like

quitting she encouraged me to continue.

Special thanks to my niece Amanda Vaughn for

proofreading and helping me edit this book and making it

presentable. After she proofread it I made changes to it;

so any incorrect grammatical or spelling errors belong to

me.

The Successful Failure

Prelude

This book existence was created from a random thought that formed the beginning of an idea that turned into a dream that was so transparent I almost let it fade away without it ever becoming an actuality. It started out so silent that I could not even hear it. As it grew, it thundered into a deafening roar that loudly projected itself into reality onto the pages of this book. All the struggles, trials, and triumphs I have gone through in my life have been molding and preparing me to become the person I needed to become so I could give a voice to this story. It would turn out to be a dream I did not even know existed inside of me. The title came to me nearly ten years ago while I was going through a major transitional period in my life.

For ten years this idea would lay dormant in my subconscious mind until another pivotal period in my life would awaken it back to the forefront of my conscious state of being so it could be heard. Its obsessive nature consumed my thoughts with endless chattering to be communicated with others so they could learn to transform their dreams into reality. This book's existence is to help people reach their true potential and become the person they were meant to become by showing people some of the things that we will let stop our progress. We can read all the self- help books we want on being successful and apply all those lessons to our life and still not change our life. It might be that we are letting the things we do not pay attention to stop our progress. Have you ever heard the saying "it's the little things that get

you"? Like sleeping with a fly in the room that has decided

your nose is where it wants to land and spend some time.

Until we get rid of the fly, sleeping is almost impossible.

The same concept applies to our life. Until we stop letting

the little things hinder us we cannot move forward with

our passion, dreams and goals.

Time will pass and we could end up realizing one day that we never gotten around to doing what we wanted to do. Take a chance on yourself, your life is worth it. Our past only shows what has happened in our life, not what we are capable of achieving. Go beyond all you have been taught to expect, and live the life you always wanted.

The Successful Failure

Successful failure: One who lives an existence they never wanted because they never attempted to achieve the life they wanted to live.

Prologue

The actions of people are influenced by the many circumstances surrounding their lives. People should be controlling their actions to influence the circumstances of their lives. Many people will never attempt to live the life they want to live because their current circumstances prohibit them from doing what their heart desires. They were never taught or learned how to overcome the environment they were born into. Living the life we want to live, and not the one we were born into, requires us to make an effort to follow our dreams and achieve that goal. Dreams do not become a reality because we want them to; they may become an actuality if we do the work necessary for them to have a chance of being brought into existence. The effort we put into making our dreams and goals come true will show how much we value them. The more we value our dreams, the more effort we will put into making them a reality. There are only two times in life when dreams and goals will be unattainable. The ones that were never started and the ones people gave up on before completing them. "You will never possess what you are unwilling to pursue", Mike Murdock.

People will always say it is never too late to chase your dreams, and that is not exactly the truth. The ones that require physical strength, endurance, and stamina must be completed while we still have elements of our youthfulness. Once we have aged past our prime stage of life (which is different for each one of us) we will start losing our physical and mental capabilities. We will start to become weaker and our reflexes and reasoning skills will become slower. No matter how hard we push against time it will ravage our bodies as we age. To delay the inevitable from occurring sooner than we expect we can exercise our bodies and our minds to keep them as young as possible. Depending on how healthy we kept ourselves when we were younger will greatly impact how healthy we will be when we get older. We only get one body in this lifetime so let's make sure to keep it in good working order for our entire lives.

The dreams and goals that involve our mental capabilities can be achieved much later in life than the ones that require physical participation. One of the best examples of an older person's dreams coming true would be *Colonel Sanders the founder of Kentucky Fried Chicken. He had a secret recipe for chicken that he attempted to sell to restaurants and was unsuccessful in convincing them to purchase it. So again at age sixty five, broke and on social security he started on his last career franchising his recipe for chicken. He would travel across the country cooking for restaurant owners and managers to let them taste for themselves how "finger licking good" it could be. He managed to franchise his chicken for four cents a chicken and did not even own a restaurant called Kentucky Fried Chicken at the time. Not sure he ever did. He convinced a friend Pete Harman, who had one of the largest restaurants in Salt Lake City, to start selling chicken using his recipe and it was so well liked that it was reported in the first year that it increased his business by seventy five percent. Kentucky Fried Chicken brought a fresh taste to takeout that was dominated by burger chains at the time.

It was a painter Don Anderson, hired to paint signs for this friend, who actually came up with the name Kentucky Fried Chicken. This same painter came up with the original bucket still in use today. An unknown cook came up with the idea of the classic wobbly red and white bucket signs that are the trademark of Kentucky Fried Chicken. This cook would later on become a successful entrepreneur himself and open up his own restaurant named after his daughter Wendy. This cook was Dave Thomas. Several years later Wendy's became one of the world's largest burger restaurant chains. Never give up your dreams because other people do not believe in them. Most people will never attempt to live the life they want to live because they are unwilling to risk everything they have for a chance to gain everything they want.

People will do what it takes to survive, but it is only the people who are willing to do more to exceed the basic fundamentals of existing are the people who will thrive. Work triumphs over talent when talent is not used to work. No matter how much talent a person has they will not reach their potential if it is not utilized. Potential without a purpose to direct our talents to make our life what we want will be wasted while we are working for other people who have a purpose for their life and are using our skills to their advantage. Our responsibilities can keep us so busy that we never have time to search out the purpose and passion that would bring the meaning in our life that we all want to have. No matter how long it takes or what we may have to go through to find it, may we all seek out the purpose that gives us a passion for our lives.

Our purpose is a lifelong calling not one time special event

in our lives that comes and passes. It will always be a part

of our being; a part so strong that we will want to share

with whoever is interested. We are responsible for our

own happiness, not how other people envision our

happiness.

The Successful Failure

Most people never plan for failure and never envisioned being successful. Most people never plan at all. People who never plan are propelling quickly towards a future with an unforeseeable conclusion. Former President Dwight Eisenhower once said "Plans are useless, planning is everything.", implying that nothing ever goes as planned, but through the planning process we can prepare for the contingencies that will arise. Life cannot go according to plan if we never made a plan for it. Without a guide to help us direct our life and navigate towards a destination we will not be able to anticipate or predict our future. Without a plan our lives will be affected by random events as they happen.

Most people who become successful; made plans to make it happen. Because successful people realize that becoming successful rarely happens by chance. They know most of the time it is made to take place by design. If we want to be successful, we will have to create a plan for a course of action that will bring about the end results we desire. Successful people either know how to or learn how to accomplish the goals they want to achieve. Knowing the end results desired and knowing how to accomplish them are two entirely different things.

Getting the desired end results we wish to have will require us to be intentional in our quest to direct our life where we want it to go. Life will   automatically follow the principle of least resistance and go in the easiest direction allowed when we are not diligent in creating the life we want to live. Unless we make a conscious effort to guide our life it will by default become the least it could have became, because it followed the easiest path possible. What we allow ourselves to settle for is what we end up receiving. Wanting more out of our life than the minimum desirability achieved will involve diligent deliberate effort from us. In order for us to create the life we want to live, we have to design our lives around ways of making it a reality.

The life we are living now is the life we have at this time chosen to live. It will not be anything more or less until we implement changes to it. The easiest and hardest thing for most people to do is change their life. We cannot have any expectations for our future other than the uncertainty of what will occur if we are not intentional in our quest to direct our lives where we want them to go. It is a directionless existence that leads to a future with an uncertain outcome. We can take control of our lives by

creating a plan of action to lead us towards the

destination of our desired end results.

Plan of Action

1] Determine what we want for our lives.

    A] How can we make it happen?

    B] Can it be done now?

    C] If not, can we learn how to make it happen?

2] Are we able to do it where we live at now?

    A] Yes- Great let's get started.

    B] No- Do we need to move to accomplish or goals? If we can do it anywhere, where would we be happiest doing it?

    C] What is keeping us from moving if that is what we wish?

3] Do we have enough money to start or finish?

A] Yes- Great let's get started.

B] No- How do we acquire the funds?

4] Making the time to do it.

A] Creating the time.

B] Being aware of time- wasters. How they prevent us from achieving our goals.

Having our plan of action completed, we now know what we want and how we are going to make it happen. We can now live intentionally instead of wandering through everyday wondering, what is the reason for our existence. We have now discovered our reason and now we can start making the life we want to live a reality. Entertaining the idea of a dream or goal without having the intention of constructing a new existence is useless if we do not follow through with action to make it an actuality. We have to control the direction of our lives if we are going to manage our future to be what we want it to become.

The best prediction for our future is to create the one we want to live. The future advances quicker than we can anticipate, disguised as the present. It materializes every second of every minute of every hour of everyday.

The dreamers, shakers, and the movers of the world who dare to live outside the normal boundaries of life realize that time passes quickly and how to make the most out of each moment before it is gone. Time is the one thing we cannot recover once it is passed. That makes time more valuable than money because we can always obtain more money. It is how we use our time, especially our spare time; that is going to make the difference in our lives. Our daily routine will determine whether or not if we will be successful. Most people will not use their spare time becoming more knowledgeable and valuable to themselves and the world. They will spend their life building someone else's dreams and will never work on obtaining their own dreams. Because ordinary people do not follow their dreams, they will accept the standards set by all the other average people. Then one day they realize time has passed them by and they never achieved what they wanted out of life. Until the fire in our soul is used for our dreams our flame will burn to light the way for other people's dreams.

Life will have many trials, tribulations, and obstacles. We might as well face them living the life we want to live because we will face them living the life we are living. To have a different life than the one we are currently living we must stop doing the same thing every day. It will require us to stop repeating the same patterns that keeps us where we are now. When we change our actions, we will change our life. We will have to break the habits that keep us tied to our old way of living. Habits direct our actions for our life more than anything else because we are the one who created them and then they take control of how we perform our everyday activities.

In order for us to change our life we must form new habits and break ourselves from the old habits that will interfere with our plans to create a new life. We must also overcome our fears of change and failure if we are to have any hope of expanding our horizons and creating a different life. Replacing our old habits with new ones requires us to change our behavior patterns. It takes about two months to form a new habit and it can take almost a year before they will become an automatic response. Until our new habits have been completely immersed into our subconscious, we will struggle against our old habits in our mindset for control of our lives. We will have to take the initiative and push through the confusion to create the reality we want or face the consequences of not taking any action. People will always create excuse after excuse to justify why they cannot change. So which are we more afraid of; changing or of our life staying exactly the same as it is now?

We have to become comfortable with being uncomfortable if we desire a different life than the one we are living now. When attempting to change our life or pursue our dreams and goals we must be willing to distance ourselves away from our comfort zone. Our comfort zone will keep us prisoners to the life we are living now, doing the same routine and things we always do. New experiences are how we grow, learn, and eventually change as individuals. Most people will never venture outside of their comfort zone to learn or do anything new. It is always easier to do what you know than to learn or do something different. It will take desire, drive, and determination to change our life or chase our dreams and goals. A person who is content does not have the ambition to work hard on creating the life they would like to live and will stay stuck in the same routine until something happens that forces them to adapt or change. We should always want to make continuous improvements in our lives.

To get something we have never had before, we must do something we have never done. Many people will never attempt to live the life they aspire to live, because they are focused on what they have to lose, not what they can gain from overcoming whatever doubts they have that has prevented them from attempting to live the life they want to live. Some are afraid to go from what they know into the realm of the unknown because it means giving up certainty for uncertainty. Fear is an emotional response developed by feelings of apprehension caused by the concern of the unknown about the outcome in the beginning of an endeavor. What is the reason behind our fearfulness? Are we worried that people will laugh and make fun of what we are doing? That we will not do well enough to succeed. We must have trust and confidence in our natural ability that it will be great enough to accomplish the task we are attempting to achieve. We are doing what we wanted to do because we felt an urge that compelled us to do it, not because we wanted other people to praise us for doing it.

So why would we let other people's opinions and condescending remarks stop us from completing what we felt an urge to accomplish. Just because other people do not understand our reasoning for doing what we wanted to accomplish, does not give them permission to stop or prevent us from obtaining our dreams and goals. We do not need anyone's permission except our own. No one else is going to live our life for us. The only people who will be interested in our lives are our family and friends. Strangers have no interest in what we do for a living or in our personal time unless it will pertain to them somehow.

It is the people in our social circle who will be the ones who help us obtain our goals, or the ones who will avert our progress to prevent us from succeeding. Our family and friends will either feed our confidence or poison our determination to accomplish our goals. The toxin they use is contagious and can infect our confidence. This poison they use to destroy our resolve is doubt. Doubt is transferred and consigned to us through our conversations with these individuals, therefore if our conviction to our goals is not resilient enough to withstand their judgement and criticism we will fail. Simple questions pertaining to our plans can create feelings of apprehension. Innocent questions such as "Can you do this?" or "Are you sure you want to do this?" have the capability to cause us to doubt our ability to achieve our goals.

Most of our family and friends want us to do well in life, but some of them do not want us to do so well that we surpass their expectations they have for their lives. We are not responsible for how other people's lives turn out, only ours. People in our social circle may maliciously avert our progress towards our goals to prevent our success. Remember that the person or persons who are obstructing our progress are our so called family and friends. This will come from the person who has a jealous/envious mindset and they see our success as a rivalry to their ego, which is caused by a competition attitude. When we exceed their expectations of our potential; we invalidate their perceived hierarchy status quo and destroy their social dominance pecking order.

These people had expectations for their life that never materialized the way they wanted and cannot envision someone they know doing better than they could have conceived themselves capable of doing. Our independence to pursue our dreams and goals will be met with apprehension from these individuals. In their minds it is a competition of whose life is better. We were never their opponents purposely living a more exciting life, or to be more successful, or out performing them in any way. We are doing the work necessary to make our life become the reality we want it to become by finding our own way in life and we will not be made to feel guilty for living the life we have chosen to live.

This will cause a dramatic shift in the dynamics of some of our personal relationships as we evolve and transform into the person we are becoming while working on our dreams and goals while aspiring to live the life we want to live. We will no longer conform to the old identity that our social circle knew and some individuals and groups we are a part of may not want to accept our new persona. They may feel that we no longer fit their standards and reject us as being an outsider. Accepting that will be hard but it is something that must happen for our greater good. We must be willing to outgrow people in our life and leave them where they are in their own lives. We must be confident in ourselves and understand that we do not always have to fit into the expectations that other people have for us. If these people are interfering and averting our progress of our transformation into our new self, it may become necessary to discontinue our relationships with these people at least temporarily.

We must be willing to remove anyone or anything from our life that is preventing us from obtaining our dreams or give up now and continuing living life as we have always lived. Family and friends should not be allowed to stop our progress on our journey of personal change and development. It is our life and we should not allow other people to control and define our limitations for us. The aspiration to improve our lives and live the dream that burns inside of us is our responsibility. Life does not happen unsystematically, it is either built intentionally by the actions we carry out or unintentionally by letting life happen with no control on our part. We have to be deliberate with dedication and perseverance if we are going to design the life we want to live. Dreams and goals may materialize through careful planning and direct implementation that is correlated on their behalf by the person or persons working to create its reality. People's lives are constructed through the actions they take or do not take to control the outcome of events in their life. We will have to purposely control our actions so we can make the end results what we want them to be.

Sitting idly by and waiting for the events in our lives to play out is no longer an option for us. Every situation that has the potential to impact our lives gives us two choices regarding how to handle the matter. We can choose to act on the opportunity presenting its self where we can attempt to direct the outcome in a favorable position that we can use to our advantage, or we can take no action while waiting for the event to play out. Taking no action is action on our part. By not taking any action we have given up our power to control the outcome and it can now create an unforeseeable conclusion. When we allow the events to play out without our input, our lives will then be controlled by the circumstances surrounding the events. During the time when we lose control of our life over to someone or something else they have the ability to influence our lives in the direction they want it to go. Until we can regain control of our lives, we are forced to react to the circumstances and that will cause long term ramifications with unpredictable results. The sooner we regain control of our life, the better off we will be by directing it in the direction we would like it to go.

Everyday random circumstances are the most common events that will influence the direction of our lives. Part of the consequences of not controlling the events, is our present and future will be affected and can return an erratic unstable outcome with unpredictable results. Our lives are our responsibility and will only return to us the results gained by the amount of effort placed into it on our behalf. Other people's actions towards our life can influence our lives for better or worse. We must choose wisely who we let into our confidence because not everyone wants us to succeed. If we are able to take preemptive steps, and we will not be able to in all circumstances, it is possible to direct the outcome of the events affecting our lives the way we would want them to go. Whenever it is possible we need to take a proactive approach to assert as much control as we can over the circumstances.

Another day must not be allowed to go by where we have not committed some kind of effort into directing our lives towards the life we want to live. All of us know that life will have moments of unpredictability that will cause a disruption in our normal everyday lives for a while. When this happens we will have to put everything on hold and attend to the disruption and react to the situation. The events affecting our life will be directing the direction our lives take by forcing us to react to the demands of the day until we are able to grasp and handle the situation and regain control of our lives. Until we are in charge again our lives will be spiraling uncontrollable and our dreams and goals are unattainable. The consequences of not being in control can have considerable significance on our life. Our future is the byproduct of our past and present moments and will return to every person the actions they deposited in those moments after amplifying everything it was given by that person. Karma explains it this way (A person's past and present actions dictates that person's future experiences.). If we want peace in the future, the past and present must be peaceful. If we want money in the future, we must invest some towards it in the past and present moments. The future cannot give us what we have not obtained. On the same token if your life is filled with drama, you will receive more drama in the future.

Creating the future we want to bring into existence and participate in is ultimately the goal we all want to accomplish. Arranging this to happen starts with us aligning our present situation to advance towards our future expectations, even though we are currently unable to meet those expectations at this time. Every action we take should be leading us towards our goal of living the life we want to live. If they are not guiding us in that direction, we need to reevaluate our process and do it differently. When we decide to act, we should move quickly with precision, intent, and with confidence that the course of action we are performing is the best option and application to use at the time.

Should the action we have taken turn out to be incorrect or insufficient we will attempt to modify and improve our decision on the matter by taking corrective action if we are able to do so. We may not be able to improve or change the action we took, so we will deal with the consequences of our decision and continue onward. Our time will not be wasted berating ourselves or complaining over a situation that did not turn out the way we wanted. Complaining does not help the situation and berating ourselves has a detrimental effect on our confidence while causing other people to have doubts in our abilities to achieve what we want to accomplish. Self-destructive behaviors will keep us from producing the results we want to achieve. We cannot expect to succeed if we are telling ourselves we are going to fail. Our minds have to believe we are going to be successful before it will happen in the physical world.

We must have confidence in ourselves and our abilities to be able to make our dreams a reality. Thomas Edison once said about the light bulb "I have not failed. I have found ten thousand ways it will not work". This is the kind of attitude and mindset we must acquire in order to make our dreams and goals a reality. We must be willing to put forth as much effort as needed for our dreams and goals to have an opportunity to become an actuality. Laziness on our part will be the reason many of us will not achieve our desired results. Our life is too important for our lack of effort to be the reason we do not succeed. If we have people helping bring about our plans, we will have to carry the workload to make sure it is done the way we have visualized. No one will work harder than we do to complete our vision. Dreams and goals start out just as ideas. An idea is just a thought to perform an action. It may be manifested into existence by intention if it is acted upon with enough determination and devotion.

It will take commitment and dedication from us to take an idea and work at it before we even recognize the potential it has to become a dream or goal we want to pursue. Our conviction requires perseverance and courage to continue on when we waver on our commitment to see our dreams and goals transpire into reality. While proceeding with our plans we will doubt ourselves and wonder if all this effort is worth it. Because the work involved will be both mentally and physically challenging and most people will talk themselves out of completing their vision. Life has a way of getting us distracted from what we wish to accomplish and then days, months, or even years can go by without us putting forth any effort towards our ambitions.

Some people will never have a dream of their own and will spend their life working for someone else at a job waiting on their retirement. These people see retirement as an ultimate goal where they will not have to work anymore and can enjoy their lives from there on out. They fail to realize that they will have gotten older over the years and will not be able to do physically what they could have done when they were younger. Also they will probably have less money since they are no longer employed in the work force and will not be able to do as many things as they thought they would be able to do. Some will be happy with the simpler life while many will not. Those of us who do not want to wait until we retire to enjoy our lives must take action as soon as possible towards the life we want to live.

We must continue undeterred in our quest if we are going to accomplish our dreams and goals no matter how the events in our life are going if we are going to succeed in creating the life we want to live. Understanding before we start that every day will be accountable to the whole project but each day will be presented as an individual day in its own regards answerable for that day's progress. A single day's occurrence should not be able to sway us from completing our tasks, no matter how great or awful the day's events turned out. Many times dreams and goals were just opportunities that people participated in for other reasons that grew into something unexpected by the participator. For many it was work that progressed, adjusted, and modified into something different than what they had prepared themselves to experience. The idea grew in the real world environment and its function grew and improved upon its self and became more than expected.

*Amazon which was founded by Jeff Bezos out of his garage in Bellevue Washington is one of the many such endeavors that have performed such actions. Jeff Bezos saw an opportunity to make money on the internet doing online retail sales. That was his original plan with Amazon and he began selling books online. In twenty three years it became the world's largest online retail sales platform for almost everything a person could purchase from the internet. It probably took years of hard work before him and his team realized that it was possible to become the largest online sales platform and started working towards making it happen. It has grown into own individual entity that no longer needs the original creator's participation to survive on its own. There are many such entities that have created their own identity out- growing the original founders and existing with new participants.

*Hewlett Packer, Google, even the Walt Disney Company started from humble beginnings and out grew the need for the creators of the companies to be present to continue on. Every one of these companies like Amazon got their start in someone's garage. All of these companies transformed from their original design and purpose into what they have become today. Hewlett Packard founded by William Hewlett and David Packard was created to produce a line of electronic testing equipment. Google was a research project of Larry Page and Sergey Brin. Walt Disney Company started as The Disney Brothers Studio was producing animated movies. *Nike founded by Phil Knight and Bill Bowerman was started to sell athletic shoes and apparel as Blue Ribbon Apparel. They would later change the name to Nike. Phil Knight would sell the items from the trunk of his green Plymouth at track events when the company was first founded.

The people who created these mega corporations were your normal average person living the same lives as most of us in the working class, attempting to make a living to support themselves and their families. Every one of them started their own businesses. They each pursued an opportunity presented to them and ended up changing their lives and ours. Success did not happen overnight; it took years of perseverance, commitment, and determination to believe in an idea and work to make it a reality. They did not let every day distractions rule their behavior and stop their progress.

Distractions will cause our attention to deviate from what needs to be accomplished and place it on something else instead of the task we were working on. Not being able to overcome distractions and stay focused on what we were doing will be the reason many people will not achieve their goals. *There was a study done by the Microsoft Corporation on attention spans. It came to the conclusion that the average human's attention span is only eight seconds long when focusing on one consecutive thought; which is shorter than a goldfish's attention span of nine seconds for a consecutive thought. Most people cannot even concentrate as long as a goldfish on one subject. It stated the suspected cause of the developmental downgrade is thought to be connected to the fast paced digital lifestyle we live in. Information overload at a quicker pace.

The modern times we live in today have many forms of distractions that cause us to lose our focus on the matter at hand and preoccupy our time. We have our families, friends, Twitter, Facebook, Instagram, television, movies, radios, concerts, sporting events, holidays, world and local news, the list could go on and on all vying for our attention and in some instances our money. These things entertain us and we enjoy them but when we allow them to take up too much of our time they will prevent us from living the life we want to life. Juvenal, a Roman philosopher, once wrote "The people are only anxious for only two things, bread and circuses." understanding to mean that most people only want two things food and entertainment. When we are distracted we are not fully engaging in the present moment event happening in front of us. The Roman Emperor in an effort to keep the subjects preoccupied and distracted, would usually sponsor gladiator battles and chariot races. These events were meant to keep the subjects entertained so they would not think about their living conditions and the taxes forced upon them, in hopes they would not organize a resistance and revolt. People purposely distracting themselves and others, has been happening since the beginning of mankind's existence.

People who spend all their free time entertaining themselves and not attempting to better their lives will never be any more than they are currently capable of being. Joe Duncan says "Your unwillingness to work on your own ideas during your free time is the reason why you have to work for someone else". Entertainment is wonderful, but when we let it control our time and life we will not achieve the potential we have inside of us. The average person is not living the life they want to live and we do not consider them to be successful. To have more than an average life, we must do things differently than the average person does. This means learning to give up everything holding us back or learning to do it differently than we have done in the past, so the results will be varied and not the same as before. To accomplish more than we ever have, we have to do more than we ever have. We will not succeed if we spend too much time working on unimportant issues not related to our goals. Our lives have to be our main focus if we are going to improve them and create the life we want to live.

There will be people in our life whose life is filled with drama and it will spill over into ours if we let it. Other peoples perceived emergencies do not constitute urgency on our part. These people will always have an urgent crisis of their own making and will cry out for help from the most stable person they know. And if we happen to be the most settled person in their life, they will call us for help in solving their dilemma. If they are capable of handling their life, we must allow them to solve their own issues to minimize the disruption they cause in ours. Many of these people have psychological issues.* NAMI[National Alliance on Mental Illness] says approximately one in five people in the United States in any given year will suffer from some sort of mental crisis. *The WHO [World Health Organization] believes the number to be higher. The WHO say one in four people in the world will have some sort of mental illness once in their lifetime.

That is roughly forty million people a year in America and out of that number nearly ten million people will suffer so severely that it will affect their daily lives. The exact reason why some people experience some kind of mental illness is not known but is attributed to being caused by psychological, biological, or environmental issues. Mental disorders have over two hundred classifications. Common ones include bipolar disorder, dementia, Alzheimer's, depression, schizophrenia, and others. Every fifth person we know or meet is dealing with some kind of mental issue we know nothing about.

Many people who seem normal by society's standards are highly functional dysfunctional people.

These people will always have drama in their life. They will always blame someone else and never accept the responsibility for their problems. They believe everyone else is out to get them and they blame everyone else for the problems in their life because they are never at peace and always stressed. They have problems that a normal functioning person will not have. Sadly many of these people will never prevail over their issues and their lives will always be chaotic. The closer we are to these individuals, the more of our time and life will be involved in caring for their well- being; connecting with these individuals can be very challenging, demanding, and in some cases burdensome. Some will withdraw from society and stay hidden in the shadows wanting contact with the outside world but afraid of what they will receive in return, while others will prefer to be left alone in solitude. These people need to know that they are loved and cared for by the people who are their caregivers and others. Then we have the people who cause strife, tension, dissension by quarreling, bickering, and disrupting everything everywhere they go.

The caregivers closest to these individuals usually have to solve or be the go in between for whatever conflict the person has created as effectively as they are able. Caring for these individuals will consume our time and energy. We must be attentive to how it affects our lives or else we will never get the opportunity to pursue our dreams and goals in order to make them an actuality. Putting our needs first is not selfish; it takes precedence over other people's priorities. If we are not taking care of ourselves, we cannot take care of other people for long. We must learn to say no to other people's propositions when it will interfere with our priorities. We are not obligated to do anything with anyone we do not wish to do, especially if it will prevent us from living the life we want to live. Our lives have to be our main focus if we are going to improve them and make them what we want them to be.

Focusing is an acquired skill that many people have not learned and it is an important part of becoming successful. Maintaining our concentration for extended periods of time requires a conscious effort on our part. It can cause the body to become both mentally and physically exhausted. We will have to train ourselves to learn how to maintain our concentration and it will take effort and time. We should not let ourselves become discouraged over our perceived lack of ability while we training our mind to become use to extended periods of exertion. Remember the principle of the law of the least resistance. Even our minds will do the least work required when not pushed by our consciousness to more than it wants to perform. We cannot become someone who does great things if we will not perform the small tasks first. This quote sums it up perfectly and I do not know who the original author of it is. "We cannot have a million dollar lifestyle with a minimum wage work ethic". When we start working on a project that we need to be completely immersed in, we should have everything we are going to need close at hand so we do not have to go searching for what we need next and become distracted by something else that catches our attention.

Some people will become distracted by the least amount of noise possible and these people prefer a quiet place so they are not disturbed by sounds. Others are deafened by the stillness of silence. Quietness to them is like a thundering roar of nothingness clouding their minds. Their ability to concentrate seems to be lost as they are processing thoughts unrelated to what they are doing so fast; they cannot comprehend in silence without a background noise to settle their mind. These people need a noise to filter the quietness to keep the stillness from absorbing their thoughts and preventing them from concentrating on what they should be applying their energy towards. We must learn to bring our thoughts back into line with what we are doing.

The art of focusing is the ability to maintain our concentration at the level needed to accomplish the assignment we are completing. Sometimes we will need to make changes in our daily routine so we are able to concentrate on our task without being disrupted. Creating the time where we will not be continuously interrupted while pursuing our dreams and goals is a major stepping stone we must overcome to make them a reality. We will need to limit distractions as much as possible. We may have to wake up earlier or go to bed later so we can decrease distractions and do the work we need to accomplish uninterrupted. That could also include disconnecting temporarily from the world by turning off our phones, computers, faxes, or anything else that could cause our attention to wander from the task at hand. No dream or goal will be obtainable until it is provided with the attention and effort it needs to prosper. It has to be made a priority in our everyday life if we are going to make them an actuality. Our aspirations must be in alignment with what we are attempting to accomplish before it will be possible to achieve it.

We could be capable of achieving much more than we currently perceive as possible if we would only do more than we currently do. Our biggest limitations are based on what we are convinced we are not able to do. It is the insecurities in our self confidence that will be what stops most of us from achieving our goals. The foundation of our self- esteem was created when we were infants, toddlers, and children by the people who were part of our environment. The praise and criticism we received from these people in our surroundings started forming our confidence and how we see ourselves compared to the rest of the world. We are a byproduct of the truth and lies we were led into believing about ourselves when we were young. Our subconscious minds were left with impressions placed on us by all the different people who had contact with us. It was the lies we believed to be true that caused the most damage to our self-esteem. The charade of who we think we are was created by how we interpreted the opinions of others about ourselves. We were all labeled by these people and those labels had a significant impact on our psyche. The labels used to define us were fat, skinny, ugly, beautiful, smart, dumb, clumsy, graceful, etc. Using these labels expressed by other people's opinions we defined ourselves by the way other people see us. These people constructed how we view ourselves and not once did we ever consider they could be wrong.

We will always end up with a distorted view of our self-esteem when we allow people to distinguish how we see ourselves, compared to other individuals. We are grading ourselves from a perceived ideal of who is greater between comparisons when we compare our self to others. When we grasp the concept that everyone is a unique individual with their own each distinctive abilities and talents and start focusing on our own original individuality we will become much happier. We are not what other people think and say about us. We are not even truly who we think we are. Actually who we are as a person, comes down to what we will do when faced with extraordinary circumstances that test our character. The people who never question their reactions to the experiences in their life will never find their true self. It is how we react to life's experiences that shape us into the person we become.

Every experience is unique to the person who goes through the event. We will all come out on the other side changed from who we were before the event happened. Our reaction to the event depends on our outlook about life in general. Our perception tends to be one dimensional, leaning towards our own understanding in regards to past experiences which shaped our attitude and current point of view towards life. Attitude is the fundamental difference in everyone's perception of the event. It depends on whether we have more of an optimist or pessimist viewpoint. Our perception of the world depends on what we consider to be normal behavior that we learned from our social dynamics.

The environment we grew up in and the one we live in now influences our point of view and what we deem acceptable in life. Our surroundings will dictate how we live and manage our lives. Our behavior is dependent on the conditions of our environment and our conduct will be responsive in a manner we think is appropriate for the circumstances at the current moment. We will be carefree and happy if we feel secure and are not concerned for our safety. If we feel like there is an element of danger, we will be defensive and cautious of the people and issues that look like they could possibility cause us harm in our vicinity. Our perspective of seeing the world as a place of opportunity or a place of struggle was formed from the environment we were raised in as children. Until we were old enough to venture away from our primary environment and experience the diversity of people for ourselves, we did not know the disparity that culture and income has on people's lives. We characterized our lives as the normal standard for everyone not realizing that the normal for our life is not the standard normal for everyone else. Our normal was created and influenced by the people in our social dynamics with whom we had daily interactions with in our life. Depending on where we were raised and lived, the social norms could have been very different from where other people were raised.

The environment in which we exist has a major influential role in how our lives will turn out. The majority of people will stay in the environment they were born into and will end up spending their whole lives there because they will never do the work necessary to make their way out of it. One cannot operate in a different environment than the one they have known, when they have not received practical contact with that environment; until they have learned to function within that environment. With limited knowledge and no actual experience in how a different environment operates people will be at a disadvantage until they obtain practical contact with that world and have adapted to the new environment they are in. The ability for people to adjust to their surroundings is one of mankind's greatest strengths. People who were born into harsh conditions such as poverty and rural areas will face many more obstacles than their wealthy counterparts and those who were born into urban areas. Those who have low incomes in rural and suburban areas deal with less job opportunities, less healthcare providers if any at all in their area, no access to higher education, transportation issues, affordable housing, etc. Relocating is usually not an option for people with low incomes because they do not have the means to support such an endeavor.

Demographic- wise more than half the world's population now lives in some sort of metropolitan area. People who live in these areas, especially the inner city face higher crime rates, congested traffic and noise, gang presence, inadequate dwellings, poverty also, etc. The people who live here do get to take advantage of things like city transportation, libraries, public parks, cultural and recreation activities that their rural counterparts do not. Thus their worldly knowledge education begins earlier and this gives them a head start in preparing for their future. Lower income children raised in a good environment in a metropolitan area have almost the same opportunities presented to them as children born into wealthier environments.

Taxes and private donations help pay for the infrastructure in metropolitan areas creating a world of opportunity that does not exist outside of the area. Most of the world's monetary resources travel through the biggest cities of the world. Most of the world's largest corporations are headquartered in a metropolitan area. Hospitals, clothing outlets, jewelry boutiques, auto dealerships, malls, grocery stores, everything a person needs to survive can be found here. All sorts of entertainment will be available in the city that will draw people from all over to participate in. There is a lot of wealth in metropolitan areas and our society regards wealth with being successful.

The wealthier a person appears to be the more successful we think they are. Appearances can be deceptive; they may give off the impression that they have a lot of wealth, but that does not mean they are not struggling with debt that we know nothing about. Successful people know one of the quickest ways to fail is to submerge under the weight of debt. A person who uses debt as a tool for being successful can be just one incident away from losing their control over the debt they are juggling. Drop one ball and it starts unravelling the complex situation they have wound themselves in; spinning their lives out of their control. Worrying over money is one of leading causes of stress.

Having money does not equate to having happiness. A person can have lots of money and not be happy, while also a person with little or no money can be happy and enjoying their life. Money is deemed so important in today's society that people will spend many hours working each week to acquire it. Doing a job that does not give them fulfillment or makes them happy. Our quest for money is as primitive an urge to us today as the quest for food and water was to our prehistoric ancestors. They could not survive and thrive unless they found food and water for everyday use, until they learned how to preserve it to use later. In modern times without money we cannot function, what most of us consider normal properly. We use money to purchase food, housing, cars, and the other items we believe are necessities for life. We also use it to buy the things we want to make our life more enjoyable.

If we are not cautious in our endeavors to acquire money; we will let the desire to possess it control our actions for obtaining it. We will have to make sacrifices of our time, family, friends, things we want to do to acquire money. When money is our main focus; we will begin rationalizing the sacrifices we are making as necessities in order to achieve more and more money. People can become so enamored in making money that their whole life can pass by without them taking the time to enjoy living. "When we do not sacrifice for the things we want, the things we want become the sacrifice" Author unknown. People will sacrifice their dreams and goals when they are content living the life they are living even though it is not the life they want to live.

People who are content with their lives usually do not change anything unless forced to do so by events or circumstances that cause their life to change. It is always easier to move by our own freewill, than being forced to change by being pressured into making a move we did not want to make at the time we had to make it. Sometimes being forced to move can be the best thing that happens to us; because we would not have moved on our own. Most people feel secure in their normal everyday routine and will not change even though they have the desire for their life to be different. Many hope their life will be different without actually doing anything to make it happen. We must want more than what we currently have before we will take any action to acquire more than what we have now. Discontentment is the start of any change; without it we will not begin progressing with any action to make changes happen. When changing our life, we need to do something so drastic that it will have such a momentous impact that it causes substantial changes to our normal everyday life. When that happens there will be no turning back to our old life. Sometimes to get what we want we must be willing to give up what we have now for an opportunity at something different.

Most people will just end up settling for how their life is now because after it is all said and done they believe their life is reasonably good. What we settle for is what we end up with. Is that the best we can hope for, that our life turns out okay? Mediocracy at best where life is just average, nothing special, just existing through time. No! We should not just settle and be content to being average. We have one life to live and we should live it to our fullest ability. Some people want it to happen, some people wish for it, while very few others will actually work to make it happen. There is a saying at the gym. "You cannot cheat the grind." Which means the results we get will come from the amount of work we are willing put into it. That is true for life also. We cannot coast through life and expect to excel. There is no sitting back and waiting for outstanding events to happen to us, we will have to get busy working to create them and make them happen.

Love this quote from Kes LaGuerre: "If you go after dreams, life will be hard. If you do not go after your dreams, life will be hard. But only one will allow you to end up living a purposeful fulfilled life." Our lives are our responsibility and to improve them or change them from what they are now, we have to take action to make them different. Young people who are starting out in life after high school or college lives are in a constant state of change for a short while. They may transition from the family structure in which they belonged, to being an individual with only themselves to care for, back to a family structure of their own making. Most will get jobs, move and leave the comforts of the family home and start their own life away from their parents, siblings, and old friends they grew up with. It is a new experience that will start to shape the rest of their lives. This time frame is probably one of the most pivotal points in a young person's life.

This time frame is an opportunity that they will never have again to do or become whatever they desire without facing the major repercussions an older person whose life is already established would endure. If you have nothing to lose and risk it all for a dream, you have not lost anything if it does not work out, but if it does work out you have created a life many people would have loved to have had. A sad truth that it seems many young people fail to understand and realize is just because they have a diploma or GED is that they have just met most employer's minimum standards for being employed by that company. It is actually only one step above being uneducated. Basically it shows that you can be trained and can learn to do the basics for the job you applied for, if you can meet the other requirements for the position. When people get hired for a position with a company they tend to get a false sense of security from being employed.

They seem to think as long as they come to work every day and do a good day's work that they will be shown appreciation and possibly promoted over the years of their service within the company. They fail to realize that the security that they think they have is controlled by someone in a higher position of authority over them. The larger the company; the more people it will have in authority over their advancement with the corporation. If one person in authority over us decides for some reason we do not meet the requirements they want in a person to advance, we will be passed over for promotions that we think we deserve, unless we can prove it is being deliberately done by this person. On the other hand just because we think we should be entitled to some sort of promotion does not mean that the company sees it that way.

Our personal life can affect our opportunities presented at work when we have things going on in our private life that reflects in our attitude at work. Everyone who works for a company cannot be promoted into a higher position and some do not want the responsibility associated with management. We cannot advance if there are no advancement opportunities available. We can waste years waiting for an advancement that will never happen. Many people cannot comprehend that they may do the same job they started out doing on day one their entire working career. If that does not sound appealing to us, we will have to be prepared to make our own way in life so that our life is what we want it to be.

Jack Ma is a Chinese business magnate, investor, and philanthropist and he explains work in an interesting way. He says "If you put bananas and money in front of monkeys; monkeys will always choose the bananas because they do not realize that money can buy a lot of bananas. In reality, if you offer a job and business to people, they would choose job because most people do not know that business can bring more money than wages. Profit is better than wages, for wages can make you a living but profits can bring you a fortune."

Never forget that the company we work for owes us nothing more if they have paid us for the time of service we have put in working on their behalf. We agreed to provide a service for a certain amount of money in exchange for our labor. What we have done, is sell our free time to the company for our wages. We are replaceable at any given time and the company has the right to lay off employees or shut down when it is convenient for them. Not only that but they can change our schedule anytime they see a need to change and it will disrupt our lives out of our regular routine. Knowing this should be reason enough for us all to live the life we want to live. Most people will never attempt to leave the job they work at because they are focused on the benefits they are currently receiving from working, not what they can gain by doing something different. It is hard to give up what we know and have been doing for years even if we realize that it is no longer beneficial to our common good.

Familiarity overrules the possibilities of the unknown. People will stay at jobs that they know are not good for their physical, mental, and emotional health long after they know they should do something different. The reasons many will stay varies from person to person. Some stay for health care coverage, the pay, vacation time, seniority, etc. Past generations use to find one job and work at it all of their life until they retired. They would then receive a pension from the company for their many years of service they provided and then live out the rest of their years in the neighborhood where they lived while working. The company paid pension plan is quickly becoming a relic of the past. Many companies have already done away with the company pension plan and have replaced them with personal retirement plans like a 401K plan.

Personal retirement plans can be transferable from one company to another company; as long as the company a person is going to be working for has a plan in place so it can be transferred. This means that people are not as concerned today as they would have been in the past about changing jobs because of their retirement. The younger generation understands this concept more clearly than the older generation and it provides them the freedom to search for opportunities that they are more passionate about and find more fulfilling to them. If they feel that their potential and talents are not being utilized in a way that gives them a sense of accomplishment, they are more likely to pursue other avenues of employment. The older generation may not leave because they fear change, or afraid they may not find another job, or do not want to spend their energy and time searching for something different. Staying at a place because you are comfortable but not fulfilled will make the hours spent working at what you do seem to have no real value. Spend years doing it and you will like you wasted your potential, talents and life at a job just to make money. If you are not looking forward to going to work in the morning, and you cannot wait until you leave at night; why are you there? "Doing the same thing over and over and expecting different results is insanity." Albert Einstein.

Doing something different requires us to acquire and apply new information to our lives. Every time we learn something new we modify our brains and improve our critical thinking skills. We actually become the information with which we supply our minds. We can be no more or less than the way we think. People who want to change their life but learn and do nothing different will always fail at it until they alter their old way of thinking with new information. When our minds are supplied with new knowledge it changes us from the person we were into the person we are becoming. When our brains learn, they build new connections between the neurons, replacing some of the connections we lose due to aging. Our brains rewire themselves over time and our reasoning skills change as we age. We will not be the same person we are now as this occurs. It is impossible to change and stay the same.

Changing is the easiest/hardest thing we can do. How we gather the new information to begin our transformation is also very easy. What we watch, read, listen to, and with whom we associate has to be different for us to be taught anything new. Our brain will grow new connections by reading, playing games hobbies, building things, anything that is not repetitive in nature forces the brain to adapt, as it learns what it did not know before. Physical exercise helps our brains by improving memory and critical thinking skills. Traveling is also beneficial for our minds by boosting creativity. Experiencing different cultures requires us to think differently than we normally would think, as we experience life presented in such a way that we never encountered before.

We learn that no matter where in the world we go that everyone is basically the same, but different. They go to school, work, have families just like us but their idea of normal is not our idea of normal. We are usually on vacation when we travel so the people we are most likely to meet will have jobs relating to the tourism industry in some form or fashion. Their job may be being a goat herder on a farm in the middle of some enchanting location, or they could be a towel boy or girl in a resort. This is their way to earn a living, to put themselves through college, or to earn extra money for whatever they desire. Just like back home doing our normal routine we go to our regular job to do earn money to make a living, buy what we want, pay for expenses and vacations. When we travel we become more open to doing new things and that mindset is brought home with us, so we are more open to attempting things we have never done when we come back home. Traveling also helps improve our moods and mental clarity.

While being away from our normal routine we are able to contemplate our lives and truly understand what is important to us. We become less fearful as we travel doing activities that are outside of our normal comfort zone. Traveling increases our patience as we wait for buses, taxis, train, planes, monorails or other methods of travel. We are away from our daily routine while traveling and this creates endless possibilities open to happen for us that do not exist during our normal day. That creates a sense of wonderment and joy for the possibility of new adventures awaiting us. So when the opportunity to travel presents itself we should act upon it and go. It will rejuvenate our spirit while giving us something to look forward to and a memory to look back on when it is over.

We do not have to travel the world to get these benefits; just removing ourselves from our everyday routine is beneficial in helping our brains rewire and grow new neutron passage ways. *Our brains are amazing; they are the most complexed living machine that has ever existed. Brains will even attempt to heal themselves after suffering a traumatic injury. The brain weighs roughly three pounds and most of its mass is water. It will use twenty percent of the body's blood and oxygen. The brain will eat itself if it is lacking in food for energy. Extreme dieting can cause the brain to eat away at its mass. Sleep deprivation has adverse effects on our brains by affecting memory, moods, impairing our judgement, and reducing our reaction times to outside influences.

Drinking excessive amounts of alcohol has the same effect as sleep deprivation and can block the brain's ability to create memories temporarily, which is why we do not remember what happened after a night of binge drinking. Alcohol can destroy neutron transmitters connecting the brain cells to one another, which is like having a car with bad spark plug wires. The connecters are not receiving the transmission of energy it needs so the car jumps and sputters. When our brains are not getting signal connections correctly it is because faulty neuron transmitters, which can lead to a breakdown of chemical imbalances within our bodies and wreak havoc to our system. On the other hand listening to music can release dopamine (the "feel good chemical"), the same chemical released when eating, exercising, and having sex. The brain also removes irrelevant information it deems unusable to help keep the brains plasticity. Plasticity is the ability of the nervous system to rewire the connections in the brain. Simply speaking the brain discharges information it no longer sees a purpose for so it can create storage for information it deems more important to our lives. It also removes useful information that we no longer use such as the algebra we learned in school. We can fill our brains so full of useless information that our brain thinks is important to our lives that it replaces actual information that we need to have available to us. One way to stop it from removing important information for more storage is to stop ingesting pointless knowledge. Another way is to keep the brain active in learning, as the old adage goes: use it or lose it.

The use it or lose it principal applies to almost all aspects of life, especially opportunities. When attempting to live our dreams every opportunity presented to us could have the potential to improve our life. It will create a set of circumstances that will change our life if we act on it, even if it does not turn out the way we wanted. Many times in life opportunities will only come around once and when they have past, the chance to acquire it is gone forever. We have to stay observant so that they will not slip by unnoticed. Lost and missed opportunities keep many people living an ordinary life instead of an extraordinary one. Opportunities are often missed because of our inability to grasp the magnitude of our actions in the present moment. Apprehension due to being afraid that it will not work out will keep many people from taking the chance presented to them. Many people want the easy way out and do not realize it is only through our hard work by creating the life we want to live that life becomes easy. Laziness on our part will never allow us to achieve our goals or produce the life we want to live. We cannot expect a wonderful life if we are unwilling to work to create it.

A lot of people are living the same day over and over and think this is living but it is not. It is existing! It is breathing and eating and staying alive to keep doing the same thing day in and out. Some people will drift aimlessly floating wherever life takes them. Just living life as it happens, never concerned about the consequences until they happen. The movie Groundhog Day starring Bill Murray is a dramatic comedy that shows this concept using humor. Bill Murray plays a disgruntled weatherman sent on location to do a live weather report while filming Punxsutawney Phil the groundhog. His character gets stuck repeating the day over and over. At first he becomes desperate to escape this reality, but as the movie progresses he accepts it and starts improving his life and the lives of those around him. He learns to make the most out of his circumstances while becoming caring and compassionate. Just like in the movie, we have to accept where we are and begin our transformation from this point. We will have to take advantage of every opportunity presented to us if we are stuck in a repetitive pattern in hopes that it will open up other avenues of change for our life.

The opportunities we get in life will come from other people unless we can create them for ourselves. Recognizing that most will come from other people, we should realize the image we portray to the world, is the one the world will judge us by. Our sense of style must be acceptable to those with whom we will have interactions or people will feel alienated by our appearance and we will lose opportunities. We hold ourselves back by believing everyone is like us and our personal image should not matter but it does. People are reluctant to be with people who seem different than their normal peers. If we have altered our looks where the impression we give is outside the boundaries of acceptability, we need to be prepared to encounter backlash over it; realizing that it will cause us to lose opportunities. The more presentable we are with our looks, speech and communicating skills the more opportunities will be available to us. People who can speak fluently and coherently will be given more attention and thus it creates more opportunities for them. All other skills we have separate us from the crowd and make each one of us valuable in our own way.

The events and circumstances that have created our present situation are irrelevant now. It is the past and we cannot change what has happened. We do have control over the present, which shapes our future. Our future is going to turn out one of two ways. It will be what we let happen, or what we made happen. If we do not take control, it will be whatever happens. We cannot stop the consequences of our past from influencing our future completely, but we may be able to lessen the impact that they may have on our lives by changing the future we were headed towards. In order to do that, we must believe in two concepts. First our future does not have to be the same as our past. Second is it is up to us to change it and make it happen. We will only be able to make it happen after we have convinced ourselves we can. It will start with a struggle in our mind of what is now and how we envision the future being.

We will have to overcome any self-doubts we have about creating a different life and then start working towards the future we want to create. When we start we will have an idea of what the end result is supposed to be, but more than likely our vision will change many times before it is completed. Our dreams and goals will never materialize until we take the action needed to make them an actuality. The sooner we start, the closer we are to completing them. Even if we do not have everything we need at this moment to accomplish them, we can go ahead and set them in motion if we can acquire what we need when we need it to complete the next step of our plan. Many people will never start because they see no way to go on to the next phase in their plan from their current circumstances. They fail to realize that the next step is not available until they take the first step towards their goal.

The fate of many people will be living the life they think they should be living due to the conditioning of the environment they grew up in, even though they desire something different. Not feeling fulfilled in life has never been the motivation they needed, to question their existence to do more to feel fulfilled in life. This is the destiny of people who were taught what to think instead of how to think for their selves. People can always be controlled by the people who taught them what they should think, if they never learn how to think for themselves. When a person learns to how to form their own thoughts they are no longer controllable by others. The person in control of their own thoughts cannot be influenced by the opinion of others when it goes against their judgement. Thus they have become their own individual identity apart from the masses. They have learned that other people should never indicate a choice of action for them, but are wise enough to seek out advice when needed. Their goal should be to always choose an action that directly correlates with the end results they desire.

Dreams, goals, and achievements are hard to accomplish or everyone would succeed at fulfilling theirs and they would be nothing more than regular day occurrences. It is when they become strenuous that we must become vigorous in our intent to stay committed to our task at hand. It is easy to fail, but it takes hard work to be successful. It is in the effort we put towards our dreams and goals that we will produce our greatest self.

Many people will never strive to become the greatest version of themselves because of the struggle and work involved to become more than they are now. Some will never push themselves to their limits and will never reach their full potential, because they are unwilling to give a little extra of themselves. Others do not know how to unleash their inner power to bring out their best, while others are prevented from advancing by people who have kept them from developing into the most exceptional version of their own selves. People who never achieve their potential are underachievers who have been prevented from developing into the person they are capable of becoming. Most people whom this has happened to have never found a suitable purpose for their lives that will give them the sustained energy they need, so that they desire to become more fulfilled. No one else can force another person to reach their full potential. It is a mental, emotional, and physical job for everyone who attempts to become more than they ever expected to be.

Reaching our full potential is a journey of self-enlightenment that begins when a person decides that they want to become more than what they have ever been before. It can take years for a person to realize the life they are currently living is not the life they want to be living. Even after knowing and understanding that the circumstances of their life has brought them to this point in life. They will question their own desire to change even after they perceive what they currently doing will not lead them where they want to go.

Author Notes

The author was born in Birmingham Alabama and currently resides in Cleveland Alabama. He wrote this book, in his spare time over the last year, while working at the job he has kept for twenty eight years. It was done to help inspire people to follow their dreams. This is the first book he has ever written. He has created a page on Facebook with the same title for people to leave comments about their failure to success stories. Comments about the book or any insights to help other people succeed.

To Become

Successful: Make a plan for our life.

Unsuccessful: Let life happen without directing it to where we want it to go.

Successful: Always learning to become better.

Unsuccessful: Never obtains new knowledge.

Successful: Wiling to change so they can adjust to the conditions necessary for becoming successful.

Unsuccessful: Stays in their comfort zone where everything stays the same.

Successful: Calculates the risks involved and are not afraid to take them.

Unsuccessful: See risks as obstacles and unwilling to face them to acquire what they need to become successful.

Successful: Willing to put forth as much effort as need to accomplish their goals.

Unsuccessful: Lazy unwilling to work.

Successful: Removes people and things from their life that hinders their progress.

Unsuccessful: Values connections more than progress.

Successful: Never berates themselves for making a mistake. They accept the consequences and will continue working for the end result.

Unsuccessful: Puts themselves and their teammates down for making mistakes, always looking to place the blame on someone else.

Successful: When the going gets tough, they struggle through and make things happen.

Unsuccessful: Quit once things get hard and out of their comfort zone.

Successful: Attentive to the tasks at hand.

Unsuccessful: Lack luster in the efforts to achieve the results they wish to achieve.

Successful: Realizes the end result is the main reason for doing what they are doing, not the financial gains.

Unsuccessful: Chases the money not the dream. Money controls their actions.

Successful: Knows perception controls the outcome.

Unsuccessful: Believes it is due to luck, good or bad.

Successful: Does not let circumstances control life.

Unsuccessful: Circumstances control their life.

Glossary

Successful: One who completes an action or a plan.

Failure: Lacks success. Never completes the required action to be successful.

Underachiever: One who never reaches their full potential.

Lazy: Unwilling to do the work necessary to complete a task.

Contentment: State of happiness or satisfaction, does not attempt to improve.

Circumstances: A fact or condition connected to an event or action.

Self-confidence: Ability to see ones worth or value.

Discipline: Training that corrects, molds, or perfects the mental faculties or moral character.

Quitter: Person who gives up easily or does not have the mindset to complete a task.

Goals: Define what you wish to accomplish.

Environment: Surroundings in which a person lives or operates.

Distraction: Anything that takes our attention away from the task at hand.

Potential: The ability to change and or grow into something better.

References

Colonel Sander's Kentucky Fried Chicken Story-The Balance

https//www.thebalance.com>Small Businesses>Franchises>Popular Franchises

Here are 10 of the Worlds Biggest Companies That Were Started in a Garage

www.scoopwhoop.com/ 10 biggest companies that started in a garage.

Nike, Inc.-Wikipedia

Https//en.wikipedia.org/wiki/Niki, Inc.

Science: You Now Have a Shorter Attention Span Than a Goldfish/ Time

time.com> Health> Neuroscience

NAMI{National Alliance on Mental Illness}

www.nami.org

Mental disorders affect one in four people-WHO

www.who.int/whr/2001/media_centre/press_release/en/

20 Fun Facts about the Brain.

https://examinedexistence.com>blog>Brain Health

Functionality.

Made in the USA
Columbia, SC
26 April 2018